T0405402

The Adventure Tarot

A ROAD TRIP—INSPIRED DECK
FOR SELF-DISCOVERY & BELONGING

ELIZABETH SU
ARTWORK BY JENNY CHANG

Andrews McMeel
PUBLISHING®

Andrews McMeel Publishing
a division of Andrews McMeel Universal
1130 Walnut Street, Kansas City, Missouri 64106

www.andrewsmcmeel.com

24 25 26 27 28 RLP 10 9 8 7 6 5 4 3 2 1

ISBN: 978-1-5248-7977-8

Editor: Patty Rice
Art Director: Holly Swayne
Production Editor: Elizabeth A. Garcia
Production Manager: Tamara Haus

ATTENTION: SCHOOLS AND BUSINESSES
Andrews McMeel books are available at quantity discounts
with bulk purchase for educational, business, or sales
promotional use. For information, please e-mail the
Andrews McMeel Publishing Special Sales Department:
sales@amuniversal.com.

To Little E:

who never stopped trying to find
where she belonged

Contents

Love Note
FROM THE AUTHOR

Ahhhh!! Hi! Hello! Welcome!

I am SO happy that you found your way to this deck. Or that this deck found its way to you. That, for whatever reason, the cosmos brought us together so we could hang out. Magic is in the air!

Now feels like the perfect time to invite you to tune in to your heart and ask yourself: What am I hoping to receive from The Adventure Tarot?

This is a deck that celebrates all aspects of ourselves: the parts we love, the parts that make us cringe, the parts we wish to cultivate, the parts we have yet to discover. Because being human is a complex experience. We are never just one thing. There is never just one perspective. So, on any given day, this deck may serve a different purpose. Let the cards reveal the truths that are meant to be seen.

I've got lots of fun goodies in store for you here in this guidebook. My hope is that it helps deepen your understanding of the cards and serves as an empowering companion on your journey.

And with that, if you're ready, take my hand, and LET'S GO ON AN ADVENTURE TOGETHER!

xo,

Elizabeth

Before You Dive In!

If you're too excited (trust me, I get it!), go ahead and skip to the fun part of playing with the cards! Maybe wash your hands, give the cards a quick smudge, or spritz something yummy in the air first. :) It's always nice to greet your cards from a fresh place.

If you think you can wait a sec, there are a couple of things I'd love to tell you about the deck:

+ **Let Your Intuition Lead the Way**—in my experience, the less I have to rely on a tarot guidebook, the better. I mean, don't get me wrong. There are a lot of great nuggets of wisdom packed inside this guidebook. But we've designed the cards to be as intuitive as possible so you can focus your energy on tapping into the symbolism instead of flipping through a million pages trying to figure out what the heck you're looking at!

For example, each suit in the Minor Arcana has a primary color palette and landscape features that correspond to the element it embodies. The Major Arcana has its own recognizable vibe. Nature imagery is deliberately used throughout the deck to draw out the emotions of each card and access the universal wisdom we all have about living in our natural world.

Let me give you a lay of the land:

Card Family	Suit	Element	Color Palette	Landscape	Deals with ...
Major Arcana (22 cards)		Spirit	Golds and silvers	The Great Outdoors	Deep questions, the collective, your soul's journey
Minor Arcana (56 cards)	Wands	Fire	Reds and pinks	Deserts and canyons	Passion, purpose, creative expression
	Cups	Water	Blues	Bodies of water	Emotions, relationships, the heart
	Swords	Air	Purples	Mountains and sky	Thoughts, decisions, the analytical mind
	Pentacles	Earth	Greens	Trees and plants	Stability, abundance, making sh*t happen

+ **The Court Cards Got Woke**—I'm not a huge fan of the gendered hierarchy of traditional court cards (*cough* patriarchy *cough*), so we chose to rename them and give them a more modern flair:

Old Name	New Name	Vibe in The Adventure Tarot
Page	Scout	Carefree High Schooler
Knight	Backpacker	Sassy Teen
Queen	Explorer	College Senior
King	Guide	Mature Thirties

+ **Say Hello to the Acrobat!**—The Hanged Man is the only card in the Major Arcana that we changed the name of because, TBH, I can't deal with the idea of, well, *a hanged man*. So, be on the lookout for an adorable and fun Acrobat instead!

✦ **Get Ready for Some Fresh Interpretations—**
I don't believe that tarot is a place for fear, shame, and/or guilt, so we've put a lot of care in infusing compassion into every card. The hope is that none of them leaves you feeling yucky!

Also! To help anchor you in these fresh interpretations, we've assigned each card an "Essence" or a loose theme to think about as you work with it. And in place of a warning for when a card is reversed, we've indicated what each card is "Releasing" to offer a gentler approach for examining what lurks in the shadows.

The Adventure Tarot is all about illuminating aspects of yourself or a situation that yearns for attention. It is not fortune-telling. While I trust that the cards always have something important to say, we are cocreating with the Universe every second of every day, so nothing is set in stone. We have free will. Choices. Power over our own destiny.

✦ **Don't Worry About Reversals**—I purposefully did not provide any guidance about how a card might have a different message if it's drawn upside down or "reversed" because, I'll be real with you, reversals confuse the sh*t out of me. I feel like it's a big accomplishment if I can just nail down one set of interpretations, so introducing a whole new framework kinda makes me want to poke my eyeballs out. However, if reversals are your jam, feel free to focus on the "Releasing" words, or allow your intuition to guide you to an interpretation of a reversed card that makes sense to you in this context. Otherwise, you have my permission to forget about them!

✦ **Take What Resonates, and Leave the Rest**—it is very important to me that you know that I do not have all the answers. Everything I share in the guidebook is written through my own lens of the world, lessons from *my* lived experience. It is not Truth with a capital T. If something resonates, wonderful! If it doesn't and you choose to toss it in the garbage, I'm celebrating that, too! The entire mission of this deck is to help you connect with YOU. I honor and trust all of your individual journeys. ·

GETTING IN THE ZONE

I fantasize on the reg about being that witchy tarot person who sits down for a reading at every phase of the moon, surrounded by candles and incense and crystal grids and flower petals of every color. But alas, that is not me. As much as I love a good ritual, I've come to terms with the fact that I'm more of a tarot-on-the-go kinda gal. I bring my deck with me to the park. I do readings with friends at coffee shops. I pull cards whenever I have a free moment: in the car, on the plane, in between meetings, while scarfing down breakfast.

What I mean to say is this is not a *precious* process. We don't have to get all heady about it. We don't need to wait for the perfect time or have #allthethings. There are no rules for communicating with the Universe. So "get in the zone," however that may look for you!

SAMPLE SPREADS

As most things go in my spiritual practice, if something is too complicated, I'm either not gonna do it or I'll overthink it and get frustrated. In case this is you, too, here are some of my go-to ways of using tarot that I hope help you weave it into your day in a fun and stress-free way!

ONE-CARD PULL: INTENTIONS

One-card pull!

I'm all about those one-card pulls. I love how quick and easy they are, how you can get guidance in an instant and not think too much about it. Here are some ways that I like to approach the one-card pulls:

◆ Set an intention for the day/week/month.

+ Reflect on an introspective question like: What lessons am I learning right now? What's the wisdom to be gained from this experience? What am I letting go of?

+ Wrap up a client session or team meeting with a card to clarify the most potent takeaway.

+ Keep it loosey-goosey and simply ask the ancestors for clarity.

TWO-CARD SPREAD: DECISIONS

What is the energy if I say YES?　　What is the energy if I say NO?

Listen. Decisions are not my thing. Just picking out a flavor of ice cream makes me panicky. But thanks to tarot, I've cut way back on the number of unhelpful opinions I seek when I'm at a crossroads, and it's been a g a m e c h a n g e r. One of my fave ways of using tarot for intuitive decision-making is to anchor in whatever choice I'm trying to make and lay two cards out. Then, I ask myself: *What is the energy if I say YES?* (and flip one of the cards over). And then: *What is the energy if I say NO?* (and flip the other card over). I am often surprised to learn that I actually *do* know how to move forward when I feel how the decision lands in my body!

THREE-CARD SPREAD: PAST, PRESENT, FUTURE

Past   Present   Future

This one is great for birthdays, transitions, endings, and beginnings. It's a powerful one to weave into client sessions, too. I like to lay three cards out, symbolizing where you've been, where you are now, and where you're headed. It's fun to see what conversations unfold when we look at the journey as a whole!

FOUR-CARD SPREAD: SEASONS

| Fall | Winter | Spring | Summer |

Since we're a nature-loving bunch—this is The Adventure Tarot, after all!—I couldn't *not* include a spread inspired by the seasons. Enter: the four-card seasonal spread. I like to think of seasons as chapters of our lives, a reminder that life is not linear and that ebbs and flows are a natural part of being human. To tap into all of these parts of ourselves and the cycles of our journey, I recommend laying out four cards in a circle (fall, winter, spring, summer) and asking what medicine there is to learn from each season.

For example:

✦ **Fall:** What am I shedding?

✦ **Winter:** What's ready to emerge from the darkness?

✦ **Spring:** What seeds am I planting?

✦ **Summer:** What am I celebrating?

Remember, these are just suggestions, a starting place. There is no right or wrong way to do this. At the end of the day, tarot is simply a tool for hearing your own intuition.

Have fun with it! Play! Let yourself be free!

Wisdom from the Cards

Major Arcana

THE FOOL

0
THE FOOL

Essence: New Adventure
Releasing: Convention

Pack your bags, crank up the tunes, put the kombucha in the cooler . . . because you're about to embark on an epic adventure! We don't know where the road will take you yet, but isn't heading into the unknown half the fun? The Fool card is all about leaps of faith. It's about answering "the call" even though you may have no idea what it means or how you'll get there or who's involved or *whyyyyyyyyyyy*. We love The Fool because she's full of best friend energy and can help us focus on all the good that comes with betting on ourselves. It takes a lot of guts to break away from the norm. People may roll their eyes or pepper you with questions because THEY. JUST. DON'T. GET. IT., but The Fool's here to say: Who the hell cares?! This card brings with it a zest for life and a desire to take control of the steering wheel. If not now, then when? As card zero, this is the beginning before the beginning. Taking any risk is scary. Now's the time to decide what risk is worth taking.

THE MAGICIAN

I
THE MAGICIAN

Essence: Synchronicity
Releasing: White Knuckling

The Magician speaks to divine synchronicities and, wow, what an *exhale* it is to be reminded of the magic around us, the relief of not having to do EVERYTHING on our own. These are moments of divine intervention where something good happens that you can't quite explain. Like when you need to find a new apartment and *poof!* the perfect one comes on the market. Or when you want to make a little extra cash and *poof!* a great opportunity falls into your lap. Or when your car breaks down and *poof!* a Good Samaritan pulls over to help. The Magician is here with a comforting message: You are not alone on your journey. If you keep showing up and doing the work, the Universe will meet you halfway. It's the idea that everything is working in your favor. With the glittery energy of The Magician, we can stop white knuckling through life, because we are constantly being supported by the Big U. When one door closes, another opens. Here, we see a collection of camping gear, representing the divine support available to you at any time. All you have to do is be open to it. Ask for what you need, and look out for signs of magic. Miracles are all around you!

THE HIGH PRIESTESS

2
THE HIGH PRIESTESS

Essence: Intuition
Releasing: Rational Mind

The High Priestess is a legit mystic. She symbolizes our seers, our healers, our psychics, our mediums, our shamans, our witches, the ability for all of us to communicate with the Divine. The High Priestess is in touch with what lies beyond the rational mind, our five senses, the naked eye. Her mantra is: I'll see it when I believe it. She is receptive to what she feels in her body, to the flashes of insight that seem to come out of nowhere, to the messages she receives in her dreams, to the art that flows through her, to the knowledge she possesses from unexplainable sources, to the ancestors who speak to her in nature. This card shows up when the veil between the earth plane and spirit plane is thin and we have greater access to the realms beyond. This is a time of heightened awareness, so pay close attention to the clues around you and the ways the Universe is offering guidance. It's a perfect opportunity to say a prayer, make a wish, or tap into your intuition. Magic is in the air.

THE EMPRESS

3

THE EMPRESS

Essence: Nourish
Releasing: Productivity

Our society forgets that we are living beings. That we aren't robots. That we weren't put on this planet to be productivity machines. Forgets that we have emotions and off days and physical ailments and a body to take care of. Burnout is what happens when we try to move through life detached from our humanness. It's like putting ourselves in the middle of a desert in the blistering sun without any water, any nourishment. We will shrivel up and die. The Empress reminds us that we *must* figure out what nourishes us and prioritize it like our life depends on it. Because, in many ways, it does. This card carries some cautionary energy. We can only go on for so long acting like we're invincible before our body and spirit begin to break down. With the guidance of The Empress, we identify where in our lives we're physically and spiritually *parched* and take steps to create more harmony. Look to our Empress for ideas on how to love on yourself today. What is your soul craving? What areas of your life need watering? How can you tend to your body with greater intention?

THE EMPEROR

4

THE EMPEROR

Essence: Self-Worth
Releasing: Hustling

The Emperor is all about uncoupling your self-worth from money and often shows up in the low moments, when we're feeling like a complete and utter failure. In the start-up world, this season of darkness is often referred to as "the trough of sorrow"—every entrepreneur goes through it. It's the FML moment when you are suddenly convinced that you've made a terrible mistake, will never succeed, and should, without a doubt, throw in the towel. This may not be the first time you've been in the trough of sorrow, but it can feel just as dark. Most people talk about this period in retrospect, when they are back on the top of the roller coaster. But The Emperor is down in the trenches with you, reminding you that we are all familiar with this exceptionally unglamorous side of the journey, and as hard as it might be to believe at the moment: The. Sun. Will. Shine. Again. In a world obsessed with hustle porn and ranking people based on their wealth, it can feel damn near impossible to feel good about yourself if you aren't constantly doing more, earning more, and achieving more. But it's all a lie! You are already perfect and whole and deserving of love JUST BY EXISTING.

THE HIEROPHANT

5

THE HIEROPHANT

Essence: Wisdom
Releasing: Quick Fixes

The Hierophant exudes grandmother energy. She's got that kind of sage wisdom that can only be gained by living. She embodies our elders, our ancestors, our spirit guides. This card has a way of showing up when we're scrambling for quick fixes. When we're certain that if only we had another degree or certification or book or healer in our lives, *then* we'd have our sh*t figured out. The Hierophant is wholly uninterested in this kind of knowledge. What she cares about is the wisdom that's already within us. Cues from our body. Visions. Ancestral connections. Past experiences that have made a home in our cells, passed from one generation to the next. The Hierophant represents the type of mentor who recognizes that we are all experts of our own lives and sees her role as merely helping you understand yourself better. She is a great ally in those desperate times when we're grasping for anything and anyone to make us feel better. Call on her when you need guidance. She won't tell you what to do but will light the path to help you find your own way out of the darkness.

THE LOVERS

6
THE LOVERS

Essence: Co-Regulation
Releasing: Catastrophizing

Ahhh, The Lovers. This card is steeped in warm and fuzzies. It highlights the power of leaning on those around us and the growth that can happen inside of our relationships. Loving someone is not always easy—arguments happen, old wounds are triggered, compromises are made. Enter: The Lovers! With this card on your side, you're able to look at these bumps in the road as opportunities to heal. There's a reason why the people we're closest to force us to confront the most shadowy parts of ourselves. The cool part is they are also in the unique position to help us move through it. This is the journey to . . . drumroll . . . secure attachment, baby! The crème de la crème. This card brings to light the sacred role of co-regulation, the ability of one person's nervous system to help regulate another's. Sometimes we get so activated that the only thing that seems to help is a good hug or a warm hand to hold or someone to wipe the tears from our eyes. The wisdom of this card is that we need to experience healthy co-regulation before we can self-soothe. The Lovers are here to challenge the idea that we can't love someone else until we learn to love ourselves. Because the truth is, under the right circumstances, the two are one and the same.

THE CHARIOT

7
THE CHARIOT

Essence: Spaciousness
Releasing: FOMO

Many of us have been hoping, praying, wishing for the day the world would listen to Asian Americans and now that it's finally here, by means of one horrific tragedy after the next, we only have the energy to binge-watch K-dramas and/or take a nap. But our bodies are whirring with a sense of urgency as if this is our ONE AND ONLY CHANCE to speak up and create art and *make a difference*. Helllllllo to the unforgiving energy of The Chariot. This card comes zooming in to throw us into panic mode, leaving us terrified that if we stop for a single minute to wash our face or fold our clothes or make a sandwich, we will miss out on the best opportunity we may ever get to be heard. When The Chariot is drawn, it's time to invite in more spaciousness. Take a cue from the woman sledding in this card. She's just doing her own thing and giving herself the space she needs to enjoy the ride. The most valuable piece of advice when The Chariot appears is: There. Is. Enough. Time. Scarcity isn't real. Opportunities aren't finite. And despite everything we've been told about business, there is room for all of us.

STRENGTH

8

STRENGTH

Essence: Endurance
Releasing: Pushing

When athletes train, they don't just hit the gym and call it a day. There's a lot more that goes into it than that. They practice practice practice. They take days off and nurse injuries. They work on their mindset and visualize winning and deal with nerves and learn how to perform under pressure. The Strength card speaks to the training journey as a whole, the gradual steps needed to achieve your goal that go well beyond physical fitness. Building in time for self-care—baths, massage, nutrition, sleep, hydration—is critical to making sure you are healthy for race day. That's the medicine of the Strength card. We often forget that preparing our bodies to take on new challenges is just as much about rest as it is about pushing ourselves. It is a forever practice to find the right balance, represented by the infinity symbol in this card. There is strength in resting; resting makes you stronger. Endurance is about the long game, and if we're gonna make it to the finish line in one piece, we have to pace ourselves.

THE HERMIT

9

THE HERMIT

Essence: Recharge
Releasing: Stress

SOMETIMES WE JUST NEED TO HIBERNATE. With The Hermit, we're offered the medicine of disconnecting. It's easy to forget how much our mental health is impacted by the world around us. Emails to respond to, friends to check in on, family obligations, bills, business goals, meetings, comparisonitis, rejection, microaggressions, explaining microaggressions, second-guessing microaggressions, expectations for days. It's e x h a u s t i n g. When boundaries are hard to set (or you're simply too tired to deal), The Hermit comes in with the advice to disconnect entirely. It's only when her phone is off and she's not busying herself attending to others that The Hermit starts to find her center again. We live in an era of oversaturation. Too much information. Too many demands. Too much too much too much. Learning how to give ourselves the space we need to return to our own voice and body and rhythm and opinions is essential to our well-being. The Hermit card brings with it a rich reminder that our natural state of being is not "stressed out." We are sensitive beings in a stressful world. There is a difference.

WHEEL OF FORTUNE

10
WHEEL OF FORTUNE

Essence: Individuation
Releasing: Obligation

Family relationships are complicated AF, and the Wheel of Fortune is here to help us #breakthecycle, thank gawwwwwd. The individuation process can be grueling—learning to accept our parents as imperfect beings, reevaluating entire belief systems, acknowledging that our childhoods might not have been the picture-perfect utopia we once thought—but it can be mighty empowering to realize that we are adults now, and adults get to make their own life decisions. It's time to spread your wings and fly. Not everyone's gonna be on board, because when one person changes, it disrupts the whole family system. But this is intergenerational trauma work. This is how we shift the course of the lineage. With the Wheel of Fortune, we're given the courage to free ourselves from toxic obligation and become our own person. Just because you played a certain role in your family growing up doesn't mean you have to hold on to it. Just because you love your parents doesn't mean you need to put up with disrespectful behavior. Just because your ancestors did things a certain way doesn't mean you need to follow suit. Let this card guide you in following your own inner compass.

JUSTICE

II
JUSTICE

Essence: Duality
Releasing: Labels

When you straddle multiple worlds (hi, it's all of us), it can be hard to know where you belong. Like, for me, being mixed-race, I often feel too Asian for whites and too white for Asians, constantly figuring out how to feel "enough" in a world that seems committed to slicing me up. This is the vibe of the Justice card. Having your feet in two boats while trying to make room for duality. You can be both privileged and oppressed. You can be white-passing and still experience racial trauma. You can feel grateful and let down at the same time. You can identify one way today and another tomorrow. If you're dizzy running around in circles trying to find your people or tired of giving a dissertation on your existence or on the verge of ripping into two because your identities are pulling you in different directions, you're in luck because the Justice card is here to help you feel whole again. The labels that society gives us are not what creates an identity. What creates an identity is a knowing in your heart, a feeling in your bones. You never have to earn the right to be who you are.

THE ACROBAT

12

THE ACROBAT

Essence: Adaptable
Releasing: Complacent

If you can't laugh, you'll cry. The Acrobat comes cartwheeling into your sphere with a little bit of levity. We *cannot* take the journey too seriously; otherwise it will, a thousand percent, crush us. The Acrobat embodies the kind of wanderlust spirit of your early twenties—THE! WORLD! IS! MY! OYSTER!—and we looooove to see it. She's not waiting around if something doesn't feel good, because srsly . . . life is too damn short. The medicine of this card is the ability to be adaptable. Things won't always go our way, and we have to be able to a d j u s t. The Acrobat is an amazing observer and helps us identify where in our life we could stand to be more flexible. With her energy, we have greater mental agility, seeing beyond black-and-white thinking, staying open to life's endless possibilities. This is the card to turn to when you need a love nudge that you're exactly where you're meant to be. You are not behind. You are not too late. Life is unfolding in perfect timing.

DEATH

13
DEATH

Essence: Transformation
Releasing: Illusions

Dude. I always think releasing will feel light and airy, like I'm in goddamn Fern Gully dancing on sparkly lily pads or something. So when it rips through my body like a terrible flu (sometimes quite literally), I'm left breathless at how violent this process actually is. The Death card speaks to the intense nature of transformations. We're talkin' major dark night of the soul vibes. A death of an identity, a way of being, a version of ourselves that we've outgrown. The Death card shows up when we're being asked to torch it all to the ground and start over. Of course, it's never really starting over. We're constantly going through cycles, peeling back layers, diving deeper, expanding our consciousness. But the truth of this card is that the Band-Aids are no longer working. We need to make some serious changes, and the only way to do it is to set our life on fire and see what survives after the destruction. Some call this darkness depression, but perhaps it is more accurately the experience of waking up to oppression. It's time to get all existential and ask ourselves the big q's: *What's my purpose? What am I doing with my life? Who am I becoming?*

TEMPERANCE

14
TEMPERANCE

Essence: Self-Care
Releasing: Burdens

I'm tired. Are you tired? The world is a sh*t show, and some days it all feels like too much. When you're a sensitive being, you tune in to the suffering of the collective. And, holy cow, do things feel heavy lately. Whether you're tending to your own intergenerational trauma, fighting for Mama Earth, or dismantling systems of oppression, know that none of this can happen overnight. It is *imperative* that we take breaks along the way. Trust that while you're resting, someone else is doing the work so that when it's their turn to rest, you'll have the energy to tap back in. This is how we create sustainable change. This is how we practice sacred activism. This is how we avoid burnout. With Temperance, we stop carrying the weight of the world on our backs and make time for rejuvenation. Soak up the medicine of the hot springs. Do something that restores your spirit. Reconnect with joy. With this card, we're being asked to examine if our current actions for social change are supportive of our own health and well-being. We all have unique roles in this revolution, and it's time to get clear on what yours is.

THE DEVIL

15
THE DEVIL

Essence: Intersectionality
Releasing: Invalidation

Listen. White supremacy taught us that some people's suffering is more important than others. It's a trap! Pitting marginalized groups against each other is a tactic, a way to keep us distracted fighting each other instead of fighting together against The System. We all know how icky it feels to be invalidated, and The Devil is the first to try to lure us into this wildly unproductive conversation. When The Devil card shows up, it's an invitation to meditate on the ways we gaslight ourselves and each other. How might you be minimizing your suffering? Do you find yourself comparing your suffering to someone else's? This card brings the concept of intersectionality to the forefront, the fact that we can have multiple identities with varying degrees of privilege and discrimination that collide with and on top of each other. We are complex beings, and there's a lot of healing that needs to be done across the board. Let's not add an additional burden to each other's plates by needing to prove that our suffering is important, that our suffering matters, that our suffering deserves airtime in the news, in books, in the classroom, in the workplace, in movies, in medicine, in therapy, and even within our own families. Any amount of suffering is too much. Let's make room for everyone to heal.

THE TOWER

16
THE TOWER

Essence: Awakening
Releasing: Sugarcoating

Well f*ck. Something has turned your world completely upside down, and now you're left to pick up the pieces. The Tower comes a knockin' to clue us in to systems that are dismantling, bodies that are remembering, relationships that are severing, and truths that need sharing. For many of us, with the rise of anti-Asian hate crimes, it was as if all of a sudden the suffering of our people that had been lingering dormant in our bodies, in our cellular memory, awakened. As if generations of cultural amnesia were wearing off, thawing, exposing things we didn't want to see, memories we didn't want to remember. While there's nothing gentle about The Tower card, it does ask us to have reverence for the process, to cycle through whatever emotions are arising—layers of sadness, disillusionment, anger, grief, helplessness, and disgust—without judgment. This card brings with it a sense of resilience, the ability to overcome adversity and fight back when faced with criticism. In the moments that feel achingly hard, the medicine of The Tower is that the Universe never gives us a lesson we can't handle.

THE STAR

17
THE STAR

Essence: Sensitive
Releasing: Numbing

Y'all, this one goes out to the empaths and Highly Sensitive People of the world, to those of us who have high highs and low lows: HAVING BIG EMOTIONS IS NOT A BAD THING. Though being called "too sensitive" is often used as a criticism, The Star card is here to help the mainstream realize that being numb ain't the gold standard we're looking for. I once learned that, back in the day, in many villages, there were Grievers who had the gift of crying for those who couldn't. They were highly respected in the community; grieving was their *job*. And when the Griever was in the midst of processing deep sorrow, the villagers would come together to take care of them—cook meals, sing songs, draw baths—because they understood that grieving was hard work, and the entire village would suffer without them. This is the vibe of The Star card. A reclamation of being emotional and a recognition of the value deep feelers bring to the collective. May our tears bring healing to all those who need them.

THE MOON

18

THE MOON

Essence: Wild
Releasing: Hiding

All hail our inner Wild Woman! Messy hair. No makeup. Brutally honest. LOUD. With The Moon card, the Wild Woman in all of us is invited to come out of the shadows and play. She symbolizes the parts of us we hide from the rest of the world, the feelings we suppress, the things we're afraid to say, the desire to break free of the cages we've been put in. Being a woman is exhausting. Being an Asian American woman is its own kind of exhausting. The Moon is our permission slip to Let. It. All. Go. No more sucking in your belly. No more apologizing for being cranky on your period. No more faking orgasms. No more laughing at jokes that aren't funny. No more appeasing and being overly accommodating and playing the peacekeeper. There is a reason why witches were burned at the stake. Society hates unruly women, women who are in touch with their own power, women whose ideas and brilliance and tenacity threaten to collapse the entire world order. The Moon card is here more than anything as a beacon of light. A reminder of all the Wild Women who have walked this path before us. They are with you in spirit, holding your hand, guiding you forward.

THE SUN

19
THE SUN

Essence: Magnetize
Releasing: Complaining

Some days, I think something is horribly wrong with me. And then the sun comes out and I remember I am just frighteningly affected by the weather. The Sun card speaks to the powerful relationship we have with our surroundings. Here, we get a lesson from our friends the sunflowers. Sunflowers always turn their heads to face the sun; they know what to do to set themselves up for success. The underlying message of The Sun card is: We can't heal in the same environment that made us sick. It's time to shake things up. Instead of focusing on what's not working, shift your attention to what is. What feeds your soul? What gives you life? Where do you feel most alive and full of posi vibes? With the energy of The Sun, we can magnetize and attract what we desire. Set an intention for yourself, pick a word you wish to embody, envision what it would feel like for this dream to come into existence, send out a prayer for what you want to call in. You are on the cusp of some pivotal shifts, and WE. ARE. HERE. FOR. IT.

JUDGMENT

20
JUDGMENT

Essence: Discernment
Releasing: Overriding Intuition

Not all healers have done their healing work. The Judgment card implores us to watch out for manipulative people who disguise themselves as spiritual teachers. The ones who get off on people's suffering, swoop in to make themselves look good, and leave you re-traumatized but call it healing so you go back for more. This is the most dangerous part of walking this path; it is vital that we do it with discernment. Spiritual leadership is a big responsibility and if healers aren't continually doing their personal work to check their biases, then they put others in danger. To lead with integrity, we *must* be committed to examining our flaws, defenses, and projections. It is a forever process. The Judgment card is here to help us walk the spiritual path cautiously and deliberately. Allow the perfectly still lake depicted in this card to act as a mirror, reflecting back the truth of a person or situation in your life. With the energy of this card, we're able to sniff out spiritual BS. We allow ourselves to trust our instincts. And, perhaps most importantly, we continue to raise our consciousness while knowing we are never "done" evolving.

THE WORLD

21
THE WORLD

Essence: Completion
Releasing: Attachment

Look around you, because dayuuum life sure is beautiful. The World symbolizes an ending of a chapter, a sense of completion, closure. There is a squishiness to it because goodbyes are hard. Perhaps some grief is surfacing; that's natural. Or maybe even a little fear, like, *Eek, what's next? What if this is as good as it gets? WHAT IF THE BEST IS BEHIND ME???* But the medicine of this card is: The journey is long, in a good way! There is so much more for you to do and explore and people to meet and magic to experience. Life is not linear, and the World card shows up to remind us of the lessons we can learn from Mother Nature, how she cycles through seasons, each serving an important purpose, a never-ending ebb and flow. What a relief it is to know that we always get to shed old layers in the fall, rest in the winter, plant new seeds in the spring, and play in the summer! We might not know exactly what lies ahead, but isn't that what makes life worth living? YOU ARE DOING IT. I AM DOING IT. WE ARE DOING IT TOGETHER.

Minor
Arcana

THE
WANDS SUIT

ACE OF WANDS

ACE OF WANDS

Essence: Excitement
Releasing: Need for Approval

HOLY F*CK! THAT'S IT! LET'S GOOOOOO! With the Ace of Wands, we have the spark of a new idea. It's not fully fleshed out yet, but we can see it in our mind's eye, we can feel it in our bodies, we know we're onto something good and it is #canteatcantsleep exciting. These are the moments that make us feel alive. The energy of the Ace of Wands is fast fast fast, so strap in tight and get ready for an epic ride. PSA: When ideas are in their baby stage, like a mama bear, we gotta be extra protective of them. Only share your idea with people who are gonna HYPE. YOU. UP. You've got an exciting vision and, sadly, not everyone will be able to follow along. It's not that your idea doesn't have merit. It's just that a lot of people can't see beyond what they already know. Don't let other people's limited capacity to dream keep you from moving forward. The Ace of Wands brings with it the reassuring mantra: My ideas matter.

TWO OF WANDS

TWO OF WANDS

Essence: Courage
Releasing: Self-Doubt

Ugh, will everyone shut up already? The Two of Wands reflects a tension between our personal dreams and the dreams others have for us. This is why the path less traveled is, well, less traveled. Most peeps don't want to deal with all the bullsh*t that comes along with going against the grain. The opinions. The unsolicited advice. The gossip. It can be a lot. But this card is here to remind you that you can handle whatever you're afraid of. So what if you fail? Sure, it will sting and be embarrassing for, like, a minute. But what if you succeed? What if things turn out even better than you expect? When the Two of Wands appears, it's time to quiet the noise around you and follow your own inner compass. Don't change who you are for a n y o n e. Here, we see a woman hiking up a mountain. She's carrying one wand in her hand, representing her commitment to her dreams, and the other wand is stuck in the ground, representing her fear of failure. See, it's not that people who follow their dreams don't have doubts. It's just that they acknowledge their doubts and do the damn thing anyway.

THREE OF WANDS

THREE OF WANDS

Essence: Logistics
Releasing: Procrastination

EYES ON THE PRIZE, BABE. Stop scrolling. Quit getting up every three seconds for a snack. You. Are. Procrastinating. The Three of Wands speaks to all the unfun things we have to do in order to reach our goals. Logistics, sales conversations, trainings, taxes, paperwork. It's all part of it. When you draw the Three of Wands, it may be time for a good ol' cognitive reframe. What are you working toward? What will following through with whatever you're putting off allow you to do? I know, I know. I hate doing boring and tedious tasks, too. The key is to break it down into bite-size pieces. Figure out the first step you can take. Jazz it up by lighting a candle or putting on some lo-fi beats. In this card, we see three friends getting ready for a BBQ. Going to the store, prepping food, cutting for days, it all takes time and effort. But it was worth it because eating yummy home-cooked food is the best. The Three of Wands is here to remind us to put up with the temporary bullsh*t so we can do the thing we actually want to do. All the work you're putting in now will pay off later, pinky swear!

FOUR OF WANDS

FOUR OF WANDS

Essence: Celebration
Releasing: Shrinking

Dayuuuum! Check you out making waves and looking radiant and being a badass! The Four of Wands speaks to our ability to let ourselves shine brightly. How comfortable are you with taking up space? With letting loose? With being *yourself*? Society has taught women, especially Asian women, to be quiet and docile. To fear being "too much." To blend into the background and wait to be spoken to and hate on our bodies and diminish our accomplishments. But guess what? This is just another form of oppression, a way to keep us playing small so we won't go changing up the systems of power. Well, f*ck that! The Four of Wands is here to remind you that you are A M A Z I N G, that your voice matters, that your happiness matters, that your existence matters. So go out there and be your brightest self possible! When we shine brightly, we give others permission to do the same.

FIVE OF WANDS

FIVE OF WANDS

Essence: Focus
Releasing: Conformity

If you keep fixating on what everyone else is doing, you are gonna completely lose your way. The Five of Wands is all about the power of focus: figuring out what advice is helpful and what's a distraction. Stop the podcasts! Unfollow the gurus! Get rid of the self-help books! There's a time and a place to take in information, and this is not one of them. You've immersed yourself in so many other peoples' ideas that you've become disconnected from your own creativity. In this card, a woman finds herself lost in a slot canyon. She'd be in for a long night if it wasn't for the five wands guiding her out. The Five of Wands offers an opportunity to reconnect with your mission and vision. *What are you passionate about? What's the legacy you want to leave? Why are you here on this planet?* The truth of this card is there is no secret to success. What works for someone else won't necessarily work for you. We all have a dharma, a soul's purpose, and it takes an incredible amount of focus, nos, and refinement to figure out what that is. You don't have to come up with the *best* idea. You just have to quiet the noise enough so you can hear the idea that you are uniquely meant to pay attention to.

SIX OF WANDS

SIX OF WANDS

Essence: Receive
Releasing: Unworthiness

The Six of Wands is comin' in hot with this encouraging message: YOU DESERVE GOOD THINGS. This card is all about receiving, allowing yourself to soak up the love and support that feels so natural to give to others. You've been working your ass off, and now you're being recognized for your efforts. This might feel uncomfortable, like it's too good to be true and you're waiting for the other shoe to drop. As best you can, try not to go there. Picking apart everything that could go wrong when something good happens is not productive. It's a defense mechanism to protect against disappointment. And if we're always trying to protect ourselves from disappointment, when do we actually get to feel happy? See, the spiritual path isn't just about healing trauma; it's also about expanding our capacity for joy. In this card, we see a woman practicing the art of receiving by relaxing by the campfire, enjoying a s'more that someone else has made for her. It feels amazing and indulgent in all the best ways possible.

SEVEN OF WANDS

SEVEN OF WANDS

Essence: Bold
Releasing: Insecurity

Truth seekers: I have some bad news. We didn't come back to this lifetime to win a popularity contest. The Seven of Wands speaks to the often lonely path of the pioneer. You see things that others can't and verbalize things that no one wants to believe. People treat you like you're the crazy one, but I promise you, sweet friend, you aren't. Don't let the haters get you down. Most of society is caught in the zeitgeist and not hip to the fact that we don't have to keep doing what's always been done. That's why you're here, to help pave the way for something new. The Seven of Wands is filled with comfort: People need to hear your truth. There's no denying that the more outspoken we are, the more backlash we'll get. We'll ruffle feathers. We'll trigger wounds. We'll see people's true colors. But for every person you piss off, there's someone else out there thinking: THANK F*CKING GOD I'M NOT ALONE. This card brings with it the courage to be bold and the resilience to get back up if you're knocked down.

EIGHT OF WANDS

EIGHT OF WANDS

Essence: Ease
Releasing: Effort

Follow! The! Ease! The Eight of Wands greets us with a nudge to take note of where we're being intuitively led. What feels fun and easy? What are we excited to work on? Where are we naturally spending our energy? These are all clues that indicate what's aligned for us at any given moment. The mind can trip us up by trying to force us to follow through with something "just because," so thank goodness the Eight of Wands is here to say: You don't have to do anything you don't want to! If something's feeling like too much, look for a way to make it easier. If you're overloaded with ideas, go with the one that carries the most energy. If you're feeling stuck, back away until you find a flow again. The medicine of the Eight of Wands is to stop pushing yourself. You may not always logically understand why you're being guided in a certain direction, and that's OK. Your job is to just listen for those nudges, ride the wave, and trust in the process.

NINE OF WANDS

NINE OF WANDS

Essence: Unapologetic
Releasing: Politeness

It's official. There are exactly zero f*cks left
to give. With the Nine of Wands, we're done
slapping a smile on our face and pretending
everything's OK. Newsflash: EVERYTHING IS NOT
OK. The world is a mess. The planet is hurting.
Injustice is everywhere. The Nine of Wands is all
about the healthy and necessary role of anger.
Anger is how we know when boundaries have
been crossed. Anger is why we change sh*t
that isn't working. Anger is what propels us to
fight for what we believe in. Anger is passion.
Many of us were taught to suppress our anger,
though, because society is uncomfortable with
angry women. Factor in the pressures of being
a ~model minority~ and you've really found
yourself with a muzzle on. The Nine of Wands
puts an end to the politeness. Here, we see
a woman who is standing in her power as a
protector, a change maker, an artist, an activist.
She is fierce and determined, on a mission.
Let her be a reminder of all the good that can
come when you say: "Enough is enough." And
remember, every time you stand up for yourself,
you are healing the wound for all of the women
in your lineage who were silenced.

TEN OF WANDS

TEN OF WANDS

Essence: Simplify
Releasing: Burnout

When the Ten of Wands appears, it's a sign that we're trying too hard. Maybe we've overextended ourselves, maybe we're overcomplicating a process, maybe we're having a challenging time delegating a project or being too cheap to get the support we need or just generally being a workaholic. Whatever it is, the message of the Ten of Wands is loud and clear: STOP TRYING TO DO THE MOST. You're burning the candle at both ends and heading straight toward burnout. Now is the time to take a look at where you're spending your time and energy and find ways to simplify. The goal here is to work smarter, not harder. There are only so many hours in the day, and sometimes it's not about getting more efficient but acknowledging when there's simply too much on your plate. In this card, we see a woman walking on a sand dune. It's barren all around her, representing the feeling of running on empty. There are ten wands scattered in front of her. She must practice ruthless prioritization—figuring out what stays and what goes—in order to make her way forward toward a more balanced and sustainable life.

SCOUT OF WANDS

SCOUT OF WANDS

Essence: Present
Releasing: Busyness

The Scout of Wands is a go-getter, a little intense, and a total blast to be around. She *lives* for the excitement of new things. There's something enchanting about doing something you've never done before, ya know? She gets a rush every time she pushes herself to her limits. No challenge is too big for her. She's happiest when she feels like she's experiencing life to its fullest. Something that can be hard for the Scout of Wands is slowing down to enjoy the present moment. She sometimes gets so busy chasing after the next big thing that she misses out on the magic that's right in front of her. Maybe it's the way the sun hits the leaves on a crisp autumn day or how her partner kisses her goodnight on the tip of her nose or the warmth of her morning coffee. As fun as the big moments are, the medicine of the Scout of Wands is to remember to appreciate the little ones, too.

BACKPACKER OF WANDS

BACKPACKER OF WANDS

Essence: Multidimensional
Releasing: Rules

YOLO, BABYYYY! The Backpacker of Wands is the cool kid on the block, always painting her nails a wacky color and ditching class to work on her art. For the Backpacker of Wands, rules don't apply. She refuses to be shoved into a box, and don't even think about trying to tell her what to do. She can be a bit of a troublemaker, but that's why we love her. She isn't afraid to go against the grain, to stand out from the crowd, to wear all black one day and polka dots the next. The Backpacker of Wands is here with the reminder that we are allowed to reinvent ourselves however many times we damn well please. We are multidimensional beings who are constantly in the process of getting to know ourselves. We can like an activity today but not tomorrow. We can take a stance for something and then change our minds. We can build a reputation in one area and decide to go in a different direction. Let our sassy Backpacker of Wands help you express yourself even more fully and give you the courage to be WHOEVER THE F*CK YOU WANT.

EXPLORER OF WANDS

EXPLORER OF WANDS

Essence: Artistry
Releasing: Censoring

The Explorer of Wands is an expert at her craft, not because some institutional body says so but because she is deeply connected to her purpose. She isn't trying to censor or sanitize or make her experiences more palatable for others. She's not focused on protecting fragile egos. She's not here to defend, justify, or explain herself. That's not the job of an artist. The job of an artist is to share their truth with the world. What the world does with it is a different story. If you're getting hand slapped by the PC police or questioning why you even bother putting yourself out there, lean on the experience of the Explorer of Wands. She's been there before. She knows all too well the sh*t you have to put up with when you speak truth to power. Look to her for support to figure out how to let go of trying to appeal to the masses so you can stay true to your art. When this card is drawn, ask yourself: *What am I called to bring to life? Who are my creations for? What was I taught about the value of creative expression?*

GUIDE OF WANDS

GUIDE OF WANDS

Essence: Go with the Flow
Releasing: Perfectionism

The Guide of Wands is mom vibes. Like, she creates the most impressive vacation itineraries and is great at coordinating a zillion tiny details, but she's also super flexible for when sh*t hits the fan (and sh*t always hits the fan). She's seen it all—the canceled flights, the cockroaches, the tent that flies away, the poison ivy, the torrential downpour, the lost luggage—and has come to expect that something will go wrong no matter how well she plans ahead. And in fact, it's through these experiences that she's learned that the unplanned moments wind up being the best parts of the adventure. Because isn't it a tad boring to know exactly what's going to happen next? The Guide of Wands shows up when we're getting a little obsessive with our plans. She clues us in to when our attachment to how things "should" go is becoming a drag and preventing us from having a good time. With the Guide of Wands on your side, you are able to accept that perfection is an illusion and open yourself up to the magic of spontaneity.

THE
CUPS SUIT

ACE OF CUPS

ACE OF CUPS

Essence: Reflection
Releasing: Self-Criticism

It's time to turn inward and have a little heart-to-heart with yourself. How are you *really* doing? What's weighing on you? What's alive for you? What feels tender and present? The Ace of Cups marks a new chapter of self-growth. Right now, it's about tuning in and listening. Don't go looking for answers yet. Cozy up with a cup of tea, still your mind, and see what arises. This is not . . . I repeat, *not*, an invitation to nitpick all the things wrong with you or your life. We're talking about loving self-reflection here, the kind where you are simply curious about your own evolution: where you've been, where you're headed, what you're leaving behind, what you desire more of. With the Ace of Cups, there's a knowing deep down inside that's ready to emerge. Your job is to listen.

TWO OF CUPS

TWO OF CUPS

Essence: Reciprocity
Releasing: Self-Abandonment

Isn't it the best when you find yourself in a relationship that feels effortless and fun? That's the energy of the Two of Cups. It's those aligned connections where there's true reciprocity, an even exchange of energy, a mutual trust and appreciation. HELL. YES. TO. THAT. Here, we see two friends paddling together on a swan boat. They each have their own boba in hand, a testament to their ability to take care of their own needs while being in connection with each other. All too often, we find ourselves in toxic, codependent patterns because that's what's familiar to us, not because it feels good. We bend over backward for other people in order to avoid the painful feelings of rejection. The Two of Cups helps us see that in healthy relationships, neither person has to abandon themselves in order to be loved and accepted. When this card is pulled, it's an invitation to examine your relationships. How supportive do they feel? How comfortable are you with advocating for your needs? What shifts need to happen in order for your relationships to feel more energetically balanced?

THREE OF CUPS

THREE OF CUPS

Essence: Belonging
Releasing: Loneliness

SWEETNESS ALERT <3 The Three of Cups is all about those slumber party vibes. I'm talkin' friendship bracelets, cucumber eye masks, dance routines, Truth or Dare—the whole nine yards! There's an innocence to the Three of Cups that makes this card kewwwwt because it taps into the younger parts of all of us who desire to belong. There's a sacredness to the bonds we share with our friends, which is why the Three of Cups often appears in times of loneliness. Maybe it's been awhile since you've had some QT with your bestie. Maybe it feels like no one really "gets you." Maybe you're in a season of transition and it's time to find new friends who you have more in common with. The medicine of this card is the reassurance that you *will* find your community. Keep putting yourself out there, lovey. Adult friendships are hard, but the more we show up in the world as our true selves, the easier it is for like-minded souls to find us!

FOUR OF CUPS

FOUR OF CUPS

Essence: Allow
Releasing: Pretending

The Four of Cups shows up when we're having a garbage kinda day. The worst! I'm sorry, boo boo. It totally sucks when things don't unfold the way we want or expect. The medicine of this card is: It's OK to be grumpy!!! The invitation with the Four of Cups is to sit with your emotions and let whatever you feel be OK. Here, we see a woman whose canoe has tipped over, her sh*t is everywhere, her belongings are floating away, things are a mess. On top of it all, everyone else seems to be having a blast, and it makes her feel ten times worse. In the Four of Cups, we allow things to be as they are. At any given moment, you may be having a completely different experience than someone else. It doesn't mean you're doing anything wrong; we're all on our own journeys. For now, be patient and give yourself permission to ignore the cups, the lessons. But in time, and with a lot of grace, gather them up, get your ass back in that canoe, and finish the damn trip.

FIVE OF CUPS

FIVE OF CUPS

Essence: Acknowledge
Releasing: Defensiveness

People aren't trying to suck on purpose, but boy does it feel like it sometimes. When emotions are high, it's natural to go into defensive mode because UGH, ISN'T IT SO OBVIOUS THAT WE ARE RIGHT?! But is it really worth playing the blame game? Most of the time, what's underneath all of the hurt is a desire to be witnessed. The Five of Cups gives us an opportunity to acknowledge our feelings, represented by the three overturned cups, while being open to another's perspective, represented by the two cups standing upright. This is not a time for problem-solving, because not all problems need a solution. Sometimes it's as simple as acknowledging that two realities can exist at the same time, a mutual respect in the face of disagreement. And let's be honest, maybe there's some merit to the feedback you're receiving . . . OOF. This card brings with it a lot of tenderness, because even if it's true, that still doesn't mean you are a terrible human. None of us are perfect. Be kind to yourself, sweet pea. There's always room for repair.

SIX OF CUPS

SIX OF CUPS

Essence: Play
Releasing: Seriousness

The Six of Cups transports us back to the days of running through sprinklers and chasing after lightning bugs and eating Fudgsicles and sipping Capri Suns. Ahhh to be a little kid again. There's something magical about those simpler times, and the Six of Cups wants to remind us that we can access that part of ourselves any time we want. When this card shows up, we're being asked to nurture our inner child and stop taking life so damn seriously. What's something you could do today just for fun? How did the younger you used to spend her time? How can you approach life with more silliness? Children are sometimes the best teachers about living in the present moment. They say what they want to say and run around in circles and giggle loudly and make weird faces and stare at butterflies and splash in puddles simply because they feel like it. Now is your opportunity to drop the adult issues for a hot sec and have some good ol' carefree fun!

SEVEN OF CUPS

SEVEN OF CUPS

Essence: Inner Knowing
Releasing: Outside Advice

Choices can signal freedom; they can also be seriously overwhelming. The Seven of Cups speaks to those big, personal decisions that only we know the answers to. Yuck. The pressure!! These are the moments when we're scrambling for someone to just tell us what to do. I'm right there with you. But always looking outside ourselves for the answer is not a very empowering way to live. The gift of the Seven of Cups is an opportunity to develop trust in yourself. I know how unsettling this can feel if you haven't spent a lot of time in spaces where your emotions were validated. But here's the thing, love. There is no one right way to do life. You're simply making the best decision you can given the information available to you. Now is the time to rinse your mind of other people's voices so you can hear the knowings of your heart. Sit by a river. Plop down in the woods. Ask for guidance from a Higher Power of your own understanding. Notice the emotions that arise. It's OK if you don't know how all the pieces fit together yet. Get curious about how something lands in your body, and let that felt sense be enough for now.

EIGHT OF CUPS

EIGHT OF CUPS

Essence: Acceptance
Releasing: Avoidance

The rose-colored glasses are off, and you're faced with a disillusioning reality. The Eight of Cups asks us to see a situation or relationship for what it is, not what we want it to be. You've ignored the red flags, dismissed the warning signs, and now, you must accept something you didn't want to believe was true. This. Hurts. Like. Hell. But, ultimately, ignorance is not bliss. Waking up is an important part of the spiritual path. You are doing the hard work. In the Eight of Cups, we see a woman kayaking in the bayou, leaving the cups—what she thought she wanted—behind. It's been a long journey, physically and emotionally, and you've made it through the worst of it. The glow of the moonlight indicates peace is just around the corner. I know it's scary to walk away from what you've known, what feels comfortable and familiar, but you have all the courage, strength, and inner resources you need to do what you know in your heart is right. Now is the time. YOU'VE GOT THIS!!!

NINE OF CUPS

NINE OF CUPS

Essence: Take a Break
Releasing: Striving

You've been at this healing thing for a while, and you know what? IT'S TIME TO TAKE A FREAKING BREAK. We can't work on ourselves nonstop; it's exhausting and unsustainable. You might not be where you want to be yet, but are any of us?! Sometimes we get so caught up in the idea of self-optimization that we forget to actually enjoy our lives. And isn't that what this journey is all about? To liberate ourselves from the grind so we can experience more pleasure? When the Nine of Cups is drawn, it's an invitation to live a little! Take a trip to Disneyland. Sign up for a pickling class. Put sprinkles on your ice cream. In this card, we see a woman floating peacefully in a swimming hole, giving her mind, body, and spirit a rest. The dragonflies are dancing in a heart, representing all the little joys we might miss when we're constantly striving for what's next. Taking breaks is a vital part of the spiritual journey, and right now might just be the perfect time to kick back and relax.

TEN OF CUPS

TEN OF CUPS

Essence: Whole
Releasing: Control

I see you and ALL that it's taken to get you to where you are today. The Ten of Cups gives us space to reflect on our journey as a whole: all that's been gained and all that's been lost. The road has not been easy, but holy sh*t. Here you are. Still standing. Still breathing. Clearer than ever about who you are. You've been tested time and time again and, damn, have you shown up for yourself or what. When the Ten of Cups appears, it's an invitation to honor your younger selves. This card speaks to that feeling of aliveness when we are finally able to move through the world as a whole person. When we've stopped rejecting parts of ourselves we don't like. When we make room for all of our emotions. When we treat ourselves with kindness. The Ten of Cups is a testament to the positive changes that can happen in our lives when we stop trying to control others and focus on our own healing. With this card, we celebrate the most important relationship of all: the one we have with ourselves.

SCOUT OF CUPS

SCOUT OF CUPS

Essence: Hope
Releasing: Jaded

The Scout of Cups is the sweeeeeetest. When she loves, she loves *hard*. She doesn't know any other way to be. She's the girl at summer camp who, on the second day, is already getting your address because she wants to be PEN PALS 4 EVA. People love being around her—she gives amazing hugs, is everyone's hype woman, and writes the best goddamn birthday cards. She's got big feelings and isn't afraid to say what's on her heart. If there's one thing she hates, it's goodbyes. In her perfect world, we'd be able to hold on to happy moments forever. The Scout of Cups embodies an innocent kind of love. The world hasn't beaten her down yet. To her, life really is full of sunshine and rainbows. If you've been feeling jaded lately, tune in to the Scout of Cups. Life has its challenges; this we know for sure. But being disappointed and cynical all the time is no way to live. Let our QT pie Scout of Cups remind you that goodness does still exist.

BACKPACKER OF CUPS

BACKPACKER OF CUPS

Essence: Brave
Releasing: What-Ifs

The Backpacker of Cups is all about being brave in the face of love. She *lives* for those cheesy rom-coms and squishy young-adult books. Talking about feelings is her favorite pastime. Some people find her moody and dramatic, but, like, some things are worth being moody and dramatic about! The Backpacker of Cups knows that putting herself out there means she could get hurt. But the amazing thing is she does it anyway. She loves with her whole heart, and it is b e a u t i f u l. To love someone—romantically or platonically—is inherently vulnerable. You never know what might happen. Maybe you'll get rejected. Maybe the relationship will dissolve unexpectedly. Maybe your heart will be broken into a million pieces. While these are all possibilities, the Backpacker of Cups is here to champion an alternative option: What if things work out even better than you could have imagined?

EXPLORER OF CUPS

EXPLORER OF CUPS

Essence: Confidence
Releasing: What People Think

The Explorer of Cups is everyone's favorite big sis. She always says hi, never makes you feel stupid, and is the go-to person for any and all questions about S-E-X. She has that kind of chill confidence that isn't about impressing others but about being secure in who she is. The Explorer of Cups is skilled at attuning to her own needs. She isn't contorting herself into a pretzel to make everyone around her happy and doesn't dim her light to make others more comfortable. With the energy of the Explorer of Cups, you're able to show up as your authentic self without constantly being impacted by other people's reactions. Sure, people might talk sh*t behind your back. Sure, people might try to make you feel small. Sure, people might flip out at you for being honest. But this card is here to prevent you from internalizing any of that and stay true to yourself. Because if you like you, then it really doesn't matter what anyone else thinks.

GUIDE OF CUPS

GUIDE OF CUPS

Essence: Boundaries
Releasing: Savior Mentality

Everyone in town looks up to the Guide of Cups. She's an esteemed midwife, is all about that fresh loose-leaf tea, and spends her Saturdays getting up impressively early to watch the sunrise. The Guide of Cups is the empowered empath we all aspire to be. She's learned how to embrace her sensitivity while staying grounded in her sense of self. This is a feat! Her superpower is setting energetic and psychic boundaries, knowing what works for her and what doesn't, and communicating her needs clearly. The flip side is the ability to respect the boundaries of others, allowing people to have their own emotional experiences, recognizing that not everything is about her! For the Guide of Cups, self-care is not a luxury but essential spiritual maintence. She knows the only way to access her highest level of wisdom is when she is in touch with her heart and spirit, not when she's running around rescuing other people. With the Guide of Cups, we see that existing as a sensitive being in a chaotic world is possible and are given the guidance we need to protect our spongy selves.

THE
SWORDS SUIT

ACE OF SWORDS

ACE OF SWORDS

Essence: Clarity
Releasing: Excuses

With Aces signifying new opportunities, the Ace of Swords offers us a chance to look at a situation with fresh eyes. So often, we find ourselves feeling trapped, like we don't have a voice, like there's no other option but to push through. But the medicine of this card is that we are not as helpless as we think. Our majestic bald eagle here gifts us with a Swiss army knife, a tool with many different functions, symbolizing the infinite possibilities available to us. Is there a conversation you've been avoiding? A relationship that no longer fits into your life? A move you need to make? Now is the time to speak your truth, mama! I know it's easier said than done, but ooo baby is it gonna feel good to advocate for yourself. You can't afford to wait any longer for something to get better on its own. We can't control other people or how they will react to us. All we can do is get clear on our own needs and express what we feel in our hearts. Ready to rip the Band-Aid off? Three, two, one, go!

TWO OF SWORDS

TWO OF SWORDS

Essence: Time-Out
Releasing: Urgency

Sometimes we're faced with a decision that's altogether too much, and we begin to s h u t d o w n. The medicine of the Two of Swords is that you don't have to figure anything out RIGHT. THIS. VERY. MINUTE. This card speaks to distress tolerance and our ability to withstand the uncomfy feelings of being caught in the messy middle. Now may not be the time to be still, as that can make the spiraling worse. Instead, consider engaging in a full-body experience. Here, we see a woman scuba diving. She's left her swords on the shore, representing her intention to take a time-out. Underwater, she can't ruminate on her thoughts because she has to focus on her breathing—inhale, exhale, repeat. Even though everything's quiet around her, the fish are still swimming, the sea turtles are still cleaning themselves, the octopuses are still scurrying about, the eels are still popping out of their hidey-holes. See, giving your mind a rest doesn't mean shutting it off; it just means directing it toward a different purpose. In time, and when you least expect it, the answers you're looking for will come to you.

THREE OF SWORDS

THREE OF SWORDS

Essence: Tender
Releasing: Logic

In the Three of Swords, it's the things said (and unsaid) that hurt the most. You have a heated argument with your partner; your friend makes a comment that stings; you feel misunderstood by your parents; hell, even your therapist can't seem to say the right thing. You simultaneously want everyone to leave you the f*ck alone and have never felt so lonely in your life. When people ask what you need, you don't know how to respond. Your mind just feels like a big swirly mess. The Three of Swords cuts right to the heart of it, represented by the three swords piercing this finger heart. The card mirrors back our internal landscape, our visceral pain, everything that can't be explained in words. Be extra gentle with yourself during this tender time. Let yourself feel the feels, or watch some stand-up comedy, or scream into a pillow, or finger paint, or lie on the grass and do nothing. Your process doesn't have to make sense to anyone (including yourself!). Getting all logical and scientific about your pain won't make it go away . . . so . . . let's not even go there. The guidance of the Three of Cups is to give yourself a little space. Distance can do wonders. Even though it might not feel like it right now, everything *will* work itself out.

FOUR OF SWORDS

FOUR OF SWORDS

Essence: Pause
Releasing: False Beliefs

STEP AWAY FROM THE TO-DO LIST . . . I REPEAT
. . . STEP AWAY FROM THE TO-DO LIST. When
the Four of Swords is pulled, it's often a sign
we've been too busy to hear our own thoughts.
This card is here to help us examine if all of the
beliefs we have about ourselves are true. Many
times, we develop narratives about who we are
based on past interactions, dysfunctional family
dynamics, and childhood wounds, and we carry
these with us into the present, even though
they have little basis in reality. A false belief
might sound like: *I don't know what I'm talking
about.* Or: *I'm a mess.* Or: *If I say what's on my
mind, I'll get in trouble.* By pausing, we can
develop awareness around these false beliefs
and take steps toward creating new, more loving
narratives. Yes, plz! In the Four of Swords, we
see a woman basking in the sun at the top of a
mountain. She's put her swords—her thoughts—
to the side and given herself permission to take
a beat and connect with her true self. This card
brings with it heaps of hope, as it's never too late
to change how you feel about yourself!

FIVE OF SWORDS

FIVE OF SWORDS

Essence: Self-Love
Releasing: Shame

It's easy to say we love ourselves when things are going well. But as soon as sh*t hits the fan and all of our triggers rise to the surface, that's when the *real* work begins. The Five of Swords is about setting our egos aside so we can practice radical self-love. I'm not talking about bubble baths and affirmations but the kind of self-love where you have to make tough decisions and swallow pride and risk humiliation. But if anything's clear about the Five of Swords, it's that now is not the time to "stick it out." In this card, we see a woman rock climbing. It's the end of the day, and her body is tired. She has the choice to either push herself to the top (illustrated by the two swords above her) or stop early (illustrated by the two swords below her). The fifth sword, in her back pocket, is a reminder that the decision is hers. Today, she practices self-love by listening to her body and calling it quits. Sometimes giving up is the kindest thing we can do for ourselves. If feelings of shame start to crop up as you make the brave decision to walk away, focus on everything that's gained by moving forward. When the Five of Swords appears, ask yourself: *Where am I pushing myself too hard?*

SIX OF SWORDS

SIX OF SWORDS

Essence: Faith
Releasing: Second-Guessing

A lot of times we get a strong intuition about something—a change we need to make, a person we need to distance ourselves from, a job we need to leave, a city we're being called to—but then our minds take over and we start second-guessing ourselves. If you've been waiting for a sign, this is it! The message of the Six of Swords is simple: There will never be the perfect time. Here, we see a woman rafting down some white-water rapids. Nothing is elegant about it, but she's still doing the damn thing. She's more focused on making it to the other side than worried if she gets some bruises along the way. When this card is pulled, you can stop all the researching and picking peoples' brains and reading self-help books and asking your friends for their opinions because none of this is actually all that helpful to you right now. You know what you need to do, and it's a matter of having faith in yourself to move forward. You may not have everything lined up exactly how you want, and there may be a thousand more things you think you need to do to feel prepared, and you may already be aware that your actions will piss someone off. DO IT ANYWAY.

SEVEN OF SWORDS

SEVEN OF SWORDS

Essence: Honesty
Releasing: People-Pleasing

Listen. I know how tempting it is to say YES to whatever comes your way, but continuing to override your intuition is gonna bite you in the ass real soon. The Seven of Swords is all about being honest. Maybe you said yes to something out of obligation. Or because you didn't want to feel left out. Or because you initially thought it would be fun but have since changed your mind. It doesn't really matter how you ended up here; the Seven of Swords gives us a chance to get out. In this card, a woman has dragged herself on a ski trip she didn't want to go on. She's brought five swords with her on the chairlift but is looking longingly at the two back at the cozy cabin, where she wishes she were instead. There are so many reasons why we people-please: trauma, attachment wounds, social norms, white supremacy, the list goes on. The important message here is that people aren't mind readers, so if something isn't sitting right, now might be an ideal time to speak up (only if it's safe, ofc).

EIGHT OF SWORDS

EIGHT OF SWORDS

Essence: Agency
Releasing: Victimhood

OK, here's the thing. Yes, racism is real, and it sucks. Yes, misogyny is real, and it sucks. Yes, capitalism is real, and it sucks. AND is there a chance you have more agency than you realize? In the Eight of Swords, we're invited to consider our personal responsibility and the ways in which we're unintentionally contributing to our suffering. We can't just blame sh*tty institutions and call it a day. That's why it's called "inner work." We have to heal our own internalized oppression just as much as we have to dismantle the systems of oppression around us. Otherwise, the oppressors continue to win because we do all the f*cking work for them. We go around censoring ourselves and policing each other and hustling for our worth. At some point, it becomes our own problem to deal with. The woman in this card is skydiving, representing her path to liberation. She's separated herself from the eight swords to declare that she will not let them rule her life. If you can't seem to shake that nagging feeling of being a victim, lean into the support of the Eight of Swords. The medicine of this card is to take back our power because, damn, do we deserve to feel free.

NINE OF SWORDS

NINE OF SWORDS

Essence: Mystery
Releasing: Fear

In the Nine of Swords, anxieties have reached epic heights. Nothing feels comfortable right now. People around you don't understand why you're making a big deal out of nothing, why you're being "irrational," why you're worrying about something that hasn't happened yet, but everything feels so real and scary in your body. Don't worry, hon, I see you. I know what it's like to be tormented by your thoughts and it is *not* fun. I absolutely despise uncertainty and when I feel like I can't see exactly how something is going to unfold, things get dark fast. In this card, a woman is alone with her thoughts, looking up at the sky. Though nighttime brings with it black widows and scorpions and other creepy crawlers, it is also the best time to marvel at the stars. See, it's not that the darkness isn't scary (because it totally is!), it's just that the darkness can hold magic as well. The Nine of Swords is a wonderful reminder of the Great Mystery of life. The unknown can feel terrifying, but isn't the idea that anything can happen also kinda exciting?

TEN OF SWORDS

TEN OF SWORDS

Essence: Integration
Releasing: Intellectualizing

F*CK BEING RESILIENT. It's exhausting to try to have our sh*t together all day, every day, and the Ten of Swords reminds us that we don't have to. This work requires so much from us, and sometimes the well runs dry. When the Ten of Swords shows up, it's a permission slip to stop analyzing your suffering. You feel sh*tty. Period. Full stop. There doesn't need to be any sort of spiritual lesson. This doesn't have to be an opportunity to do shadow work. It doesn't matter if this is about your attachment style or intergenerational trauma or being an empath or what your astrological chart says or if your chakras are aligned or your Human Design. You can just exist. Is that not a relief or what? Here, we see a woman sitting on the ground, completely spent. Her swords, scattered around her, are being buried by the falling leaves, symbolizing this period of integration. Not everything needs to be processed on an intellectual level. You've already done the hard work. Now you can just rest and let the healing take place without lifting a finger.

SCOUT OF SWORDS

SCOUT OF SWORDS

Essence: Self-Worth
Releasing: Imposter Syndrome

The Scout of Swords is all set to conquer the world when BAM! she's hit with some nasty imposter syndrome. She thinks: *Will I make a fool out of myself? Is everyone better than me? Did I talk too much? PLEASE TELL ME I DIDN'T TALK TOO MUCH.* When her insecurities kick into high gear, she feels like a worthless piece of sh*t. Research shows that one of the reasons perfectionism is so relentless is because we, perfectionists, focus on the 1 percent that could have been better versus the 99 percent that went well. We have a difficult time feeling proud of ourselves because we always think we could have done something better, communicated more clearly, not tripped over our words, asked more questions, showed more enthusiasm, showed less enthusiasm, not sounded like a robot, you get the idea. In this card, our determined Scout is embarking on her first big hiking trip. Her backpack is filled with a million different wilderness tools, symbolizing her tendency to overthink in new situations. The thing she has to remember is that making mistakes is all part of the learning process. It's not that she didn't prepare enough. It's that doing new things is hard for everyone. We're all just figuring it out as we go.

BACKPACKER OF SWORDS

BACKPACKER OF SWORDS

Essence: Differentiation
Releasing: Obedience

The Backpacker of Swords is lovable and obnoxious at the same time. She isn't trying to be the worst but, like any teen, isn't concerned about how her actions will impact others. She snaps at her parents, slams doors, lies to friends, and has a knack for arguing with teachers at the most inopportune times. But the Backpacker of Swords can teach us a thing or two about the benefits of disobedience! She embodies a sense of healthy differentiation, figuring out where she ends and other people begin. This is a vital part of the individuation process. We need to be able to question authority, to figure out what beliefs we agree with and which ones we don't, to make mistakes and learn from them, to chart our own path. With the aid of the Backpacker of Swords, we bring online the sacred skeptical part of us that doesn't automatically agree with everyone. We see words as words, not truth. We filter what people say through our own lens and observe how it lands in our body, taking what resonates and leaving the rest.

EXPLORER OF SWORDS

EXPLORER OF SWORDS

Essence: Tolerance
Releasing: Hierarchies

The Explorer of Swords is the popular girl in school who everyone is slightly terrified of. She commands the hallway like a goddess, turning heads with her gorgeous hair and glowing skin and stylish kicks. Her presence is polarizing. People either worship her or hate her. But the Explorer of Swords is a human with flaws and fears and dreams and gifts, just like the rest of us, no better or worse than the next person. This card brings to the forefront the fake hierarchies we create in our minds—believing someone is superior or inferior because of money, status, power, education, appearance, you name it. It is natural to judge (and actually an important survival skill!), but if we're constantly sh*t talking other people (hey, no judgment lmao), we start to internalize those same messages. The Explorer of Swords invites us to practice tolerance and tear down the pedestals, to remember that we're all imperfect beings walking this path together. We'll vibe with some people and not with others, and if we can accept that even people who get under our skin are worthy of love and respect, then maybe we'll be more inclined to offer that same love and respect to ourselves when we feel inadequate.

GUIDE OF SWORDS

GUIDE OF SWORDS

Essence: Mind–Body Connection
Releasing: Compartmentalizing

The Guide of Swords is a mind–body wizard. She's your Asian Auntie who's been practicing tai chi for at least three decades and is known to drop some serious truth bombs about how our physical ailments are connected to mental distress. Headaches are the result of an overactive mind. Night sweats are a form of purging past beliefs. Digestion problems relate to our ability to break down and metabolize food *and* thoughts. In traditional Chinese medicine, there are no labels like "anxiety" or "depression," no subcategory for mental health, because the mind and body are one. The Guide of Swords helps us see the big picture, how nothing is a coincidence, and gives us a break from trying to figure out *why* something has happened. If you're feeling let down by your body or pissed off about getting sick or annoyed that you're injured, tune in to the wisdom of the Guide of Swords. She's here to offer grace for the process and make sure you're tending to the health of your mind as much as your body.

THE
PENTACLES SUIT

ACE OF PENTACLES

ACE OF PENTACLES

Essence: Nurture
Releasing: Urgency

The Ace of Pentacles brings with it a gentle, nurturing energy. You are planting new seeds and that sh*t takes time to grow. It's like that phrase: An overnight success is ten years in the making. You have to be patient; you have to be prepared for a long road ahead. Maybe you'll fall on your face, or get rejected, or fail spectacularly. But one thing is for sure, you 100 percent won't succeed if you don't even try. When the Ace of Pentacles appears, it's time to throw your hat in the ring and give yourself a fighting chance! You don't need to think about what this means five years down the road. It's just about getting the wheels in motion atm. Apply for that writing residency. Dust off your resume. Make a website for your new biz. Research engineering bootcamps. Progress over perfection, mama! This card is buzzing with possibility, how will you take advantage of it?

TWO OF PENTACLES

TWO OF PENTACLES

Essence: Work/Life Balance
Releasing: Rigidity

OK, you've gone into Tasmanian devil mode. Rushing from one thing to the next, juggling ALL the balls. The Two of Pentacles is here to help you pump the brakes and make sure your basic needs are being met: Are you feeding yourself? Are you sleeping enough? Are you getting fresh air? When this card is drawn, it's a good time to reflect on how much emphasis you've been putting on work lately and if there are other parts of your life that could use some tending to. Perhaps your relationship needs some TLC. Or you haven't seen your friends in ages. Or you've put your health on the backburner. Or you're feeling disconnected from your spirituality. Despite what capitalism wants us to believe, work isn't everything. The Two of Pentacles allows us to look at our life more holistically, becoming more willing to say no to some things in order to say yes to others. This card is about work/life balance. Not the kind where you're expected to be superhuman and miraculously gain more hours in the day but the kind where you make hard choices in support of your overall well-being. We can have it all, just not all at once.

THREE OF PENTACLES

THREE OF PENTACLES

Essence: Cocreation
Releasing: Stubbornness

LOVE ME SOME COCREATION MAGIC! The Three of Pentacles is a v cute card, representing the sparkly energy of the creative process and all that comes with joining forces with the right people. It speaks to the power of working alongside those who complement you, the ones where, together, you accomplish something far greater than you could have on your own. In this card, we see three pals working together to put up a tent. They are all bringing their different strengths to the table and contributing to the larger goal in their own beautiful way. We aren't meant to do everything by ourselves, and the Three of Pentacles is here to help you manifest the talented souls destined to help you bring your big vision to life—be it a creative partner, a web developer, a marketing expert, a literary agent, an operations guru, or whatever type of support you might need. Even if you aren't clear on this yet, the Three of Pentacles will guide you in the right direction. When this card shows up, it's an indication that you're ready for that next level. If you can get comfortable with letting go of control and trusting other people to help you, the sky's the limit, baby!

FOUR OF PENTACLES

FOUR OF PENTACLES

Essence: Letting Go
Releasing: Scarcity

It's tragic. We can't hold on to people and things and places and experiences forever. The Four of Pentacles speaks to the idea of impermanence, which IMO is one of the hardest lessons of human existence. Letting go can feel brutal, like a part of you is dying. The simple act of getting rid of clothes can unearth all sorts of baggage—old memories, guilt, what-ifs, money trauma, the passage of time. There is grief in saying goodbye, a confrontation with our own mortality. That's a big reason why we hoard: We don't want to deal with all of these intense emotions. But when we stuff stuff stuff our lives full of sh*t, we suffocate. We have trouble moving on. We prevent ourselves from growing into who we're meant to be. Here, we see a backpack that is so full, the pentacles are falling out, symbolizing how you gotta get rid of the old to make room for the new. Let the Four of Pentacles help you Marie Kondo the heck out of your life. Trust me. It may suck at first, but damn is it liberating. Knowing that, when all is said and done, what you're left with is what matters most.

FIVE OF PENTACLES

FIVE OF PENTACLES

Essence: Surrender
Releasing: Gripping

Sometimes limitations are a good thing. I know, I know. It can be super annoying not to be able to be everything everywhere all at once. BUT (hear me out!) limitations can be a godsend. It's the Universe's way of swooping in when we're having trouble saying no on our own. And thank goodness for that because, eek, being pulled in all directions is draining. As a member of the Pentacles suit, this card speaks to limitations of the physical realm, such as the need to budget, pick a home base, commit to a job, take a sick day, that sort of thing. This card depicts a classic rainy day. A woman looks out the window at the five pentacles, thinking about how much it sucks that the rain messed up her plans. At the same time, she could use a day to chill, and there's relief knowing Mother Nature made the decision for her. The Five of Pentacles shows up to anchor us, to narrow down the options, to offer a sense of rootedness. It's time to surrender to "what is." You may not be happy about it, but surrender is oftentimes more about accepting discomfort than feeling good about something that's out of your control.

SIX OF PENTACLES

SIX OF PENTACLES

Essence: Resourced
Releasing: Guilt

Society has socialized women into believing that being generous is synonymous with being a good person, so to be a good person, you must be in a perpetual state of giving. Giving in every sense of the word: time, money, energy, smiles. The thing is, we can't be in a season of giving indefinitely. If we always give, our wells will run dry and there will be nothing left for when we need it. The Six of Pentacles reminds us that we deserve to feel supported and resourced, too. This card debunks the scarcity myth that our happiness somehow takes away from the happiness of someone else. It also guides us to give from a place of integrity versus performance. In this card we see a woman apple picking. She isn't immediately giving away all of her apples but rather taking what she needs first and only giving once she feels she has extra to give. If the idea of prioritizing your needs above others feels yucky, lean into the wisdom of the Six of Pentacles. This card is a great ally as you learn to love yourself in this important way.

SEVEN OF PENTACLES

SEVEN OF PENTACLES

Essence: Perseverance
Releasing: Resistance

Sometimes the lesson is to respect when you're pushing yourself too hard and stop. But in the Seven of Pentacles, the lesson is to honor the resistance and keep going. This card brings to the surface the nuance of these two experiences of discomfort and gives us the ability to discern between them. You've done all you can to nurture the seeds you've been planting, and now it's go time. YOU'RE READY, BB. In the Seven of Pentacles, we see a woman at the summit of the Grand Teton. It took e v e r y t h i n g to get her ass up that mountain, but she f*cking did it. It's not that she wasn't scared (she was) or that the conditions were perfect (they weren't). But she prepared, got the right gear, and hired someone seasoned to lead the way. As the saying goes, we don't rise to the occasion, we fall to our level of preparation. The Seven of Pentacles shows up as a boost of confidence, assuring us that, even in the face of obstacles, we'll know when to change course, when we're too far outside of our comfort zone, when the risks outweigh the reward. For now, you have all that you need to move forward. So go get 'em, tiger!

EIGHT OF PENTACLES

EIGHT OF PENTACLES

Essence: Appreciation
Releasing: Modesty

You've been over here taking it day by day, putting in the effort, giving it everything you've got, and hot damn, LOOK AT THIS LIFE YOU'VE CREATED FOR YOURSELF. You might not be where you want to be yet—the casualties of being a dreamer, amirite—but oh em gee, can you imagine what your younger self would think right now? She cannot *believe* how far you've come. The Eight of Pentacles offers you an opportunity to look back on your journey with deep appreciation for where you've been. You've made it through the fire. You stepped up to the challenges. No shortcuts. No accidents. Pure blood, sweat, and tears. Did you have help along the way? Sure. But ultimately, it was *you* who put the wheels in motion, *you* who made your dreams a reality. In this card, we see a woman who just hiked the entire twenty-four-mile Rim-to-Rim Grand Canyon trail. She's looking back at the path, thinking to herself: *Wow, how the hell did I even do that?* That's the vibe of the Eight of Pentacles: in awe of your own amazingness.

NINE OF PENTACLES

NINE OF PENTACLES

Essence: Authenticity
Releasing: Comparisonitis

The Nine of Pentacles comes with a nice big *exhale*. This card helps us appreciate that yes, we are different AND it is our greatest asset. When we are totally and completely ourselves, it doesn't matter what anyone else is doing because it has nothing to do with us. We aren't worried someone will steal our brilliant idea because how would they replicate it without us? We aren't concerned that our story has already been told because how could it be if we weren't the one to do it? We aren't comparing our successes with random people on the internet because how do we know what goes on behind the scenes? With the Nine of Pentacles, we embrace our authenticity and everything that makes us, us! In this card, we see a woman next to a rainbow eucalyptus tree, a reminder of how this magical one-of-a-kind tree isn't trying to be anyone but itself, so NEITHER. SHOULD. YOU. She's surrounded by nine pentacles, symbolizing how much effort it took to get to this place annnnnd what a sick reward it is to finally feel free to be yourself. You'd be surprised by how prosperous it is to be exactly who you are.

TEN OF PENTACLES

TEN OF PENTACLES

Essence: Meaning
Releasing: Autopilot

OK, so maybe you aren't couch surfing anymore, or maybe you occasionally splurge on cut pineapple, or maybe you even live in a place with a dishwasher AND in-unit laundry (hey, a girl can dream), but it wasn't that long ago when you didn't have any of these luxuries, and guess what? Life was good then, too! With the Ten of Pentacles, we take stock of all forms of abundance: Inside jokes. Cozy nights in. Hummingbirds. Spooning. Boba dates. Glazed donuts. Scrunchies. Summer concerts. This card grounds us in our own idea of happiness and what gives meaning to our life. Here, we see three besties on top of a camper van. There's nothing fancy about it, but this is a moment they'll cherish forever. It's easy to think "once I make this much money" or "once I hit this milestone" or "once I meet this person," *then* I'll be happy. The gift of the Ten of Pentacles is the ability to create meaning out of our lives right here, right now. If you've found yourself on autopilot lately or laser focused on WHAT'S NEXT, tap into the lessons of this card. There's so much wonderfulness around you if you stop to look!

SCOUT OF PENTACLES

SCOUT OF PENTACLES

Essence: Alignment
Releasing: Disappointing Others

If you're going on a road trip and want a guaranteed fun time, invite the Scout of Pentacles. She's your witchy friend who's never without her tarot deck, flower essences, crystals, tinctures, vision board materials . . . ya know, the essentials. She can't go anywhere without someone spilling their secrets to her because there's just something about her presence that makes people feel right at home. The challenge for the Scout of Pentacles is that she hasn't learned yet that her energy is her most precious resource. She's a bit of an emotional dumping ground atm. For the Scout of Pentacles, it's critical that she asks herself on the reg: *Does this give me energy or drain it?* When this card appears, it's a good time to take an inventory of how you're spending your time, money, *and* energy. There are a lot of energy vultures out there who will gladly take take take, so let the Scout of Pentacles help you plug those energy leaks and focus only on what's in alignment. You may disappoint others, but isn't that better than disappointing yourself?

BACKPACKER OF PENTACLES

BACKPACKER OF PENTACLES

Essence: Do Less
Releasing: Overachieving

The Backpacker of Pentacles is your edgy cousin with the pink highlights, rad tats, and envious talent to dance like a K-pop star. If she were to start a club at school, it would be "The Underachieving Club" because she really just doesn't give a sh*t. So what if she's a B student? The Backpacker of Pentacles embodies the teenage spirit of mediocrity. The satisfaction of doing the bare minimum and being fine with it. This card is *chef's kiss* about releasing the need to be an overachiever. It highlights all of the ways we push ourselves to be productive, to prove something to someone, to avoid being deemed as "bad." But being "bad" simply means falling short of the ridiculously high expectations imposed upon us (thanks, patriarchy) and the Backpacker of Pentacles says: So be it! This is the card to turn to when striving to be the best is getting pretty dang old. By embracing the laissez-faire attitude of the Backpacker of Pentacles, you give yourself permission to be lazy. You recognize when something's *good enough*. You stop trying to #LIVEYOURBESTLIFE and instead take things day by day, hour by hour, minute by minute. Because let's be real: Working hard is overrated.

EXPLORER OF PENTACLES

EXPLORER OF PENTACLES

Essence: Pleasure
Releasing: Struggle

The Explorer of Pentacles is over struggle for struggle's sake. She's had it with the drama. She's done with the treadmill. She no longer wears her stress as a badge of honor. The Explorer of Pentacles is here to e n j o y   h e r s e l f. She doesn't care how much she paid for something or what commitments were made or how prestigious an opportunity is, IF IT'S NOT A HELL YES, IT'S A HELL NO. This card brings to the surface how often we find ourselves addicted to suffering and skeptical of joy. If there's anyone who wants to rewrite this narrative for us, it's the Explorer of Pentacles. She firmly believes we're put on this planet to feel *good*. When this card appears, it's a sign to cultivate more pleasure in your life. Take a deliciously long lavender bath. Make a charcuterie board with all of the expensive cheeses. Treat yourself to a bouquet of fresh lilies from the farmer's market. Let your intuition guide you. The more pleasure we experience, the more we say f*ck you to the systems of oppression that want to keep us struggling.

GUIDE OF PENTACLES

GUIDE OF PENTACLES

Essence: Capable
Releasing: Helplessness

If there's ever an apocalypse, the Guide of Pentacles is the one you'll want by your side. She knows how to forage for mushrooms, which plants hold medicinal properties, and the secret to building a rainproof shelter. This card speaks to the gift of self-reliance, being able to trust that, no matter what life throws at you, you'll be able to take care of yourself. The energy of this card is not so much about being so fiercely independent that you reject the support of others as it is about taking matters into your own hands. Don't understand the stock market? Take a workshop on investing! Want to learn some self-defense? Sign up for a Krav Maga class! Concerned about a health issue? Schedule that doctor's appointment! The Guide of Pentacles approaches challenges head-on. She isn't waiting around for anyone to save her. This card shows up when we need a little kick in the butt to remember that we are smart, capable, and resourceful. It is a tremendous source of guidance in wobbly times. Life has a way of throwing us curveballs, and when it does, tap into the resilience of the Guide of Pentacles. She will help you find your way.

Behind the Scenes

My writing teacher once told me that, as Asian American women, we often need to write ourselves into existence. That is everything The Adventure Tarot is to me. A window into my own self-love journey, a way of declaring to the world that I AM PROUD TO BE ASIAN.

As a third-generation, mixed Chinese-white woman from a predominantly white town in the Midwest, I have spent most of my life rejecting my culture. Erasure and assimilation are their own flavors of racial trauma. The rise in anti-Asian hate crimes in 2020 hit me h a r d, as it did with many, and for the first time in my life, my Asianness felt important to me. Grief is strange like that. It's like I didn't realize what was missing until my heart felt this new kind of achiness, a longing, a loss.

At the time, my hubs and I were living nomadically, traveling all over the United States. What started out as a carefree road trip became a two-and-a-half-year search for belonging. It was through this reclamation journey that The Adventure Tarot was born.

Turns out that loving yourself is a hell of a lot easier when you can see yourself at the center of the story.

This is for you. This is for me. This is for us. <3

Warm and Fuzzies

Holy. Sh*t. We did it, fam. We created something out of nothing. Birthed a dream into being. Pinch me!!! The Adventure Tarot is the thing I worked on when I was supposed to be working on another thing, and it ended up being THE thing. Life is weird and wonderful like that. This deck has always been a project of my heart. It's a culmination of the lessons I've learned, the people I've met, the places I've seen, the tears I've cried, the magic I've experienced. It is everything good I could take from all the pain. It's a commitment to joy. My entire being is filled with profound gratitude.

To my brilliant illustrator, Jenny Chang: From the moment our paths crossed, I knew you were the one who was meant to bring this tarot deck to life. Thank you for the magic you infused into every card, for seeing the vision and purpose behind it all from the start. This is our Eight of Pentacles, and I am so very proud of us. To my witchy friend and dear agent, Margaret Danko, at High Line Literary Collective: I'M NOT CRYING, UR CRYING. Thank you for holding my hand through every step of this process. For the voice memos and pep talks and proofreads and humanness. You make me feel like anything is possible. What a gift. To Patty Rice and the entire team at Andrews McMeel: I can't think of a better place for The Adventure Tarot to call home. Thank you for believing that a tarot deck that centers Asian American women deserves to be in the world and for showering this project with such beauty and care. To my incredible team of Cali Orr, Angelina Lutsenko, and Jewel Ocampo: my OG Three of Pentacles, the lights of my life: Thank you for the daily reminder that we're doing something that matters and for making work so damn fun. ILYSM. To our Monday Vibes and Instagram communities: You've been with me since the beginning, through every Ace and every Ten. Your support and presence are sunshine.

To Stephanie Han and Anne Liu Kellor, my Hierophants. Stephanie: You always tell me to keep spreading joy. It's these words that I turn to whenever I'm worried my work is not important enough. Anne: It was in your workshops that I found my writing voice. Thank you for helping me uncover the deeper truths of my stories and heart. To Dr. Melanie Brewster, for encouraging me to keep writing and questioning. To Lexi D'Angelo: You showed me that magic and business can coexist, and it changed my life. To my Asian sisters Ahran Lee, Katie Quan, Iris Kim, Kyunghee Chen, Kristen Chuang, Rachelle Mohtadi, and the Asian American Girl Club: the beacons of light on my reclamation journey. Your work is fire; your friendship is medicine. To Hannah Cooper, Callie White, Maddie Stilley, Cassie McIntosh, Natalie Gross, Bonnie Vig, and Rachael Plitch: This path is a hell of a lot less lonely with you on it. To Mrs. J: for making Little E feel destined for greatness. To my in-laws: the best cheerleaders. To my little sister and following our own inner compasses. To my parents and ancestors: Your courage is my courage. Thank you for believing in the power of women.

To Veronica Kim: my Two of Cups for life. Thank you for showing me it's OK to fall apart, for the side-splitting laughs, for the TV recs, for every exclamation point. What would Little E do without Little V?

To my hubs, Andrew Lee: The other day, you sent me a cartoon about two dinosaurs, a red one and a blue one. The red one says, "i don't know what i'd do if i lost you," and the blue one goes, "really? i know exactly what i'd do." The red one replies, "what?" and the blue one answers: "find you." You have taught me everything I know about what it means to love and be loved. Doing life with you is my favorite adventure. Thank you for The World.

And finally, to each and every one of YOU! Thank you for being exactly who you are. For asking the big questions and living your truth. Together, we are The Moon.

Love from the Illustrator

This project has truly been a dream project for me and a huge labor of love.

Thank you, Elizabeth, for your trust and guidance the whole way through and your brilliance, creativity, and vulnerability in creating this deck. The initial pitch spoke and related to me in so many ways and I know it will also reach so many others!

Biggest thank-you to my husband, Jon, for endless late nights and unwavering support, and my Miles, who is my inspiration for everything I do.

P.S. Let's Keep This Party Going!

I'm just gonna come out and say it: I hate goodbyes LOL. So let's be friends on social! Head over to Instagram (or TikTok!), say hi, and tag me with your deck so I can celebrate all of your adventures and we can stay up-to-date on each others' journeys. :) And for some extra-cozy feels, sign up for my *Monday Vibes* newsletter at elizabethsu.com. Can't wait for all the magic to come!

:camera: @heyelizabethsu

:musical_note: @heyelizabethsu

elizabethsu.com

About the Author

Elizabeth Su, MA (she/her) is a mixed Chinese American writer, creative, and the founder of *Monday Vibes*, a newsletter focused on women's empowerment and celebrating Asian joy.

After calling it quits on her Silicon Valley career, Elizabeth earned her master's degree in clinical psychology from Columbia University, where she researched burnout and perfectionism. Her work has been featured in the *Los Angeles Times*, among others, and centers around self-love, the multifaceted nature of being human, and keeping it real on the spiritual path.

When she's not writing (or trying to smash the patriarchy), you can find her dancing in the kitchen, binge-watching teen dramedies, or finding the hottest boba spot in town.

Join the slumber party fun on Instagram and TikTok @heyelizabethsu or by signing up for her *Monday Vibes* newsletter at elizabethsu.com.

About the Illustrator

Jenny is an illustrator and designer based in NYC, currently working at *Insider* as a deputy design director. Raised in Vancouver, Canada, she graduated with a fine arts degree at the School of Visual Arts in New York. When she's not drawing, you can find her laughing at dog memes, obsessing over astrology, or overeating desserts.